MASSIMO DAMBROSIO

PAPA BEAR'S
STORIES

8+1 tales for budding
young entrepreneurs.

It was another gloriously sunny afternoon in Honey Woods.

All the little bears were happy: there were some who hid in the trees, some who played on the merry-go-rounds, and some who ate delicious honey ice cream.

Among all these bears, there was also Papa Bear and his two little twins, Ni and Vi. Papa Bear played with his children every afternoon and was happy to spend so much time with them.

One day, having just returned from the park, the twins asked Papa Bear why he had more free time than the other grown-up bears to play with them.

Papa Bear was prepared for this question, and by now his children were old enough to hear the answer.

"My dear Ni and Vi, it's true, we spend a lot of time together playing happily, but it hasn't always been like this. Before you were born, I also worked all day long collecting honey from the big hives," Papa Bear said. Intrigued, the little bears asked: "Tell us, Papa, what has changed?"

Papa Bear began to explain again: "When Mama and I discovered that we were going to become parents to two beautiful little bears, we realized that it would be nice to spend more time together as a family. I had to find a way to have more freedom from day-to-day work and always have honey in the pantry."

"So, what did you do, Papa?" Ni asked.

"I started working even harder!" Papa Bear replied.

"But, Papa! I don't understand; first you said that you wanted to work less, and now you're telling us that you worked even more!" Vi argued.

"Yes, Vi. We worked in a different manner, and more cleverly! Every night, even though I was very, very tired, Mama Bear and I would study ways to have more free time. I'll tell you the secret I discovered then: you can only have more free time if you help a lot of bears."

"That's wonderful, Papa! Tell us what you did next!" the two little bears asked.

"Well, it wasn't easy. We tried over and over again to develop lots of ideas, and we finally managed to find not one, but two, really great ideas!"

"Papa, Papa!" the twins shouted in unison.

"Yes, yes, I know what you want to ask me...but now you have to be patient, because before I tell you what we came up with, you have to listen to a few stories".

"But, Papa..." Ni and Vi protested.

"Each story has a valuable lesson, and only at the very end will you discover the common thread that ties them together. If you're patient, you'll understand why I am now a different bear than I was when I started my journey...and you will be, too. I promise!" Papa Bear replied lovingly.

"Okay, Papa, start telling us the first story right away!" said Vi.

"All right, all right, you kids are curious, huh?" Papa Bear said, chuckling. "For the first story, we'll go to Japan!"

The story of Aki:
The little monkey from Japan

In Japan, there is a community of little monkeys that live on a mountain where it is very cold.

They are lucky monkeys, because on the slopes of their mountain there are thermal water pools where they can stay warm, especially in winter.

The little monkeys love these pools and can spend hours relaxing in the steam, but first they must get permission from Takumi, their tribal leader.

Takumi is, after all, the largest and oldest monkey in the village, and everyone must respect his decisions, even Aki, our story's hero.

Aki is a young, slightly crazy little monkey with lots of ideas bouncing around in his mind, and not always successful ones: in short, he is always up to something.

Takumi often punished Aki's intemperate behavior by forbidding him to bathe in the warm pools: "Aki, when you behave like the other monkeys, you can spend more time in the warm pools," he always repeated to him.

But Aki wasn't like the other monkeys; he wanted to be himself and dreamed of having a pool all to himself.

One day, as he was mulling over a solution, he noticed that there was a small spring on one side of the mountain flowing straight downhill. Aki climbed the slope and couldn't believe his eyes: the water was warm!

He immediately had one of his typically chaotic ideas, but this one was different from the others. "What if...", he thought, "...wow, what an idea!": Aki's thoughts were racing!

To put his plan into action, Aki needed Takumi's permission, so the next day he stopped Takumi as he was walking towards the thermal pools: "Takumi, Takumi, wait!" Aki shouted excitedly.

Old Takumi turned, a little uneasy, and when he saw Aki running towards him, he brought his paw to his forehead and sighed: "Ah, poor me, what other bizarre idea has he had now?!"

As expected, Aki immediately began: "Takumi, I have a fantastic idea! To set it up, I need to use one side of the mountain, you see, that steep one right over there," he said, pointing to the area where he had climbed the day before.

"Aki, what do you want to do with it? There's nothing there for you," replied Takumi, who had an idea of his own: he wanted to teach that unruly little monkey a lesson once and for all, so he jumped at the chance.

"All right, Aki, I give you permission to use that part of the mountain, but in return, I ask you to give up bathing in the hot water pools forever," Takumi said with a stern look.

At that point, Aki thought that this agreement required a hefty price, but he was also confident that his idea was sound and that it would be successful, so without delay, he looked Takumi straight in the eye and replied: "All right, I accept your conditions. We have a deal!"

So Aki, climbing up to the spring, exclaimed: "If I work hard, I can create my own pool! I can take a bath whenever I want, without anyone forbidding me!".

This was Aki's brilliant idea, to create a pool of his own: "I will start every morning at sunrise and finish only when it's dark!" he said to himself, to give himself courage.

Days passed and Aki was always there digging, but after so much work, the rock began to shatter.

All the other monkeys watched him in astonishment: some were curious about what he was up to, and others made fun of him.

But Aki didn't care because he was focused only on his goal: "Digging is harder than I expected, but I made a commitment to myself and to Takumi, I cannot fail!".

More weeks passed and Aki's vision began to take shape: the water was finally starting to pool and wasn't flowing straight down the slope!

Even Takumi began to change his mind about Aki: "That boy is working hard, and if he keeps it up, soon his pool will be finished".

Our little monkey was almost finished when the unthinkable happened: a large landslide broke off from the mountain and the rocks filled the entire pool that he had so painstakingly dug. Aki was very sad because he saw all his hard work go up in smoke.

It was then that Takumi approached him, saying: "My dear Aki, I didn't believe in you at first, but your tenacity has made me change my mind, and now I know that you can do it. Don't give up now: moments of difficulty are a part of life. Remember that the real difference is made by those who manage to pick themselves back up again".

Aki could not believe his ears: Takumi believed in him! And so, without thinking twice, he returned to his spring and worked with so much passion
and energy that in two days the
rocks were cleared from the pool.

Aki was in seventh heaven: now he could take a dip in a pool of his own and, at long last, he threw himself into the hot water to relax after all his hard work.

Aki would not have to ask anyone for permission to go for a dip, ever again.

"My dear little bears, Aki's story contains many lessons," Papa Bear said. "First of all, the importance of knowing how to see something that others cannot see yet. Aki saw a pool where others could only see the steep slope of a mountain".

"The story also talks about the importance of hard work: Aki worked for months to have a pool all of his own. And it reminds us that we must never give up in the face of difficulties: the unexpected is part of the game of life".

"Papa, Aki took a lot of risks," said Ni.

"That's right, Ni: the most important lesson is that Aki did not trade his freedom away for anything, even when he faced the risk of not being able to bathe in his beloved thermal waters anymore," Papa Bear replied.

"Papa, what a lovely story! I also liked that Takumi and the other monkeys changed their minds about Aki," Vi added.

"It's always like this: at the beginning of your journey your friends will tell you that you shouldn't start, someone in your family will try to discourage you, thinking that they have your best interests at heart. But you shouldn't listen to them, because your actions will change their minds...just like what happened to Aki".

"Papa, Papa, tell us another story, please!" said Ni impatiently.

"All right, Ni. Now listen to me carefully because the next story will take us to Africa!"

The story of Naja:
the gazelle that saved her herd.

We find ourselves in the great African savannah. Rising in the morning, the sun illuminates and warms the great plain where thousands of animals live.

Among all these beautiful creatures is Naja, a strong young amber-colored yearling gazelle.

Naja is very close to her mother and her herd: it is thanks to them that she has survived those most difficult and dangerous first months of life.

Naja still remembers when that hungry hyena was driven away by her mother with a fighting spirit that she had never seen before, or when the herd had managed to ward off that very fast cheetah, getting her to safety.

But now Naja was almost fully grown, and she too ran swiftly and nimbly to dodge attacks from predators. So, proud and cocky, she ventured out in search of grass to eat, sometimes straying a little too far from the others.

Her mother always told her: "Naja, always follow the herd, because it is our strength and our safety. We gazelles are strong when we support each other, but alone we are weak and in danger".

Naja remembered these teachings and would do anything to save all the members of her herd if a predator approached threateningly.

The greatest dangers are found near the large water pools. The African savannah is hot: scorching, in fact, and all animals must drink if they do not want to die of thirst.

But water also hides many pitfalls: it is the place where crocodiles, the sworn enemies of gazelles, hide and attack.

All the gazelles in Naja's herd approached the pond very carefully so that if one of them heard any suspicious movement underwater, they would warn the rest of the group, allowing everyone to get to safety.

Naja had also been rescued several times by some companion who had noticed a crocodile suddenly emerging from the depths of the lake.

Unfortunately, gazelles are not as good at hearing noises in the water as they are at running and dodging predators on land, so every now and then a member of the herd would fall victim to the jaws of the huge crocodiles.

Naja was always sad when this happened, and cried all day long. She was terrified that sooner or later something bad might happen to a friend of hers or, worse, to her mother.

But Naja was a strong and courageous gazelle and was determined not to give up and to change this situation. "There must be a way for us to drink peacefully and escape those ugly beasts!" she thought all day long.

And so one morning, while she was drinking together with the whole herd, Naja noticed that there was a group of little birds that drank undisturbed in an area nearby.

A few moments later, there was a crocodile attack, which, however, was in vain because all the birds had quickly spread their wings and had flown elsewhere.

Naja had an epiphany: an idea so dazzling that the savannah sun paled in comparison.

"What if the little birds are more sensitive to the crocodiles' movements underwater than we are? By drinking where they are, we could also be warned in time," Naja reflected, "it would be the end of our fears and the crocodiles would go hungry!"

Naja observed the birds' behavior as they drank in the pond in the following days and never saw one fall victim to a crocodile, not even the fastest and most cunning ones.

Eventually, she was sure she had collected enough evidence and ran to her mother at the speed of light:

"Mom, Mom, I discovered something sensational!" and so Naja told her about what she had seen.

"Naja, we can't, it's too dangerous. We must stay close to the other gazelles, there is safety in numbers," her mother replied.

"But, Mom, this way we can finally drink safely!" Naja insisted.

"Naja, it's not up for debate, we've always done it this way, for generations. The unity of the herd is our strength and you can't allow yourself to play by your own rules as usual," her mother scolded.

However, Naja didn't want to give up: "I love the herd, too, and if there is a way to save even one gazelle, I want to try. Mom will never give me permission, so I have to sneak away and prove to everyone that my intuition is correct," she thought as she worked out her plan.

And so, the next day while everyone was drinking, Naja silently slipped away from the other gazelles and went to drink right where a group of little birds were standing nearby.

When her mother noticed that Naja had wandered off, she began to call her, terrified: "Naja, have you gone crazy?! Get back here now!! It's dangerous, you're not safe!"

But Naja was adamant in her resolve and, after a few seconds, she noticed that the little birds began to fly away, so she too, promptly moved away.

Her idea was correct: moments later an enormous crocodile came out of the water with its jaws wide open, but found nothing to bite into.

Naja's strategy had worked! And all under the incredulous eyes of her herd.

All the gazelles ran excitedly towards Naja. Even her mother, initially furious, cheered her daughter with the others.

Thanks to Naja, they had found a way to escape the deadly crocodile attacks forever, for whom there was nothing left but to shed their proverbial tears.

"And so ends this second story, my children," Papa Bear said with satisfaction.

"Ohhhh, what courage Naja had!" the twins exclaimed with admiration.

"You're right, Naja was brave but not reckless: she studied the little birds' behavior on the lake for days. She did not risk her life because first she observed carefully and then she acted".

"It's true, Papa!" said Ni.

"You see, my loves, courage is important but you must never be so reckless as to endanger your life or that of others," Papa Bear said seriously.

He added, "The first lesson of this story is that, before you embark on a venture, you must take the proper time to observe and reflect. Once you are sure, however, act quickly and vigorously, giving it your all".

"Just like Naja did!" Vi exclaimed.

"Exactly. The second lesson is that you mustn't listen to those who say 'We've always done things this way' or 'There's nothing we can do'. There is always a new way, a new path," Papa Bear explained. "Observe, think, and imagine: you will always have the opportunity to improve that which is done out of habit".

"Naja taught us a great lesson," said Vi, "Even the little ones can make a difference!".

Ni, as usual, was impatient because he wanted to hear another story, but it was beginning to get dark.

Then Papa Bear said, "All right, I will tell you one last story, but only when you are ready for bed, otherwise Mama Bear will be very angry!"

In no time at all, the twins were ready to hear their father's new story.

"My little ones, this story happened not far from Honey Woods; it tells of a fox who used her wiles in a somewhat unusual manner."

The story of the fox who no longer had to steal grapes.

Near the borders of Honey Woods there was a large vineyard, full of grapes so sweet that they were an irresistible temptation for a fox who lived nearby.

The vineyard was well cared for by a farmer who went every day to remove the weeds, prune the dry branches, and above all make sure that no one entered his precious field.

The fox was really very greedy for grapes: to her they were so beautiful and juicy that she could not resist.

So as soon as she saw the farmer move away a little, the fox would sneak into the field, steal a bunch of grapes, and then run for the hills, running the risk of being captured by the farmer.

The farmer was tired of these continuous robberies and the moles' invasions, above all. In fact, the moles dug holes that reached under the roots of the vineyard, ruining it and risking killing the vines.

So one day the farmer fenced off the field and planted several signs on the ground saying, "No foxes and moles allowed."

But in reality it was of little use: the moles continued to dig and the fox, with great cunning, snuck into their tunnels to pass beyond the fence.

One day, while the fox was in the vineyard intent on stealing a bunch of grapes, she saw a mole come out of a newly dug hole.

"Hello, mole," said the fox, "Are you also unable to resist the sweetness of these grapes?"

"Grape? Oh no!" the mole exclaimed. "It means that I got lost, I ended up in the vineyard again by mistake."

"So you're not here to eat the grapes?" asked the fox.

"Oh no, we moles do not like grapes at all. We eat earthworms, larvae and insects."

"Bleurgh," said the fox, disgusted. "But if you don't eat the grapes, then why do you moles come here? Don't you know that by digging all these holes, you ruin the roots of the plants and risk killing them and so I can no longer steal...um, eat...the grapes?"

"Ohhhh, I'm so sorry! We don't do it on purpose, but we moles are almost blind and we often get lost. If I had a way to figure out where I'm going, I wouldn't come here for sure!" the mole apologized.

"Why don't you moles wear glasses? They might help you."

But the mole had a valid reason: "We don't wear glasses while we dig because they get scratched or we lose them".

"But you can't even read the farmer's sign that prohibits entrance to moles!" the fox observed.

"Yes, you're right! If there were a way to read them, we would know that we have taken a wrong turn and we wouldn't enter the vineyard. Now I have to go, it was a pleasure to meet you." And so the mole left, digging his way along.

This meeting struck the fox greatly, who in fact left the grapes alone that day and went thoughtfully back to the woods.

"Let's consider the facts," she said to herself. "First point: moles do not like grapes. Second point: the moles do not know when they are going to enter the vineyard. Third point: if they did know, the mole said they would certainly not enter."

The fox, cunning by nature, wanted to find a way to keep those moles away forever. "This way I would help the farmer...after all, the moles are more dangerous than I am. In the end, I steal a tiny bunch of grapes, but they risk killing an entire vine!" she thought, pacing in her den.

"...and if I found a way, I could always have grapes and no longer risk my life attempting to steal them, behaving honestly. That's it!" the fox gasped.

So the fox went to the vineyard and, instead of running away, approached the farmer and said: "My friend, we are no longer enemies, I have found a way to drive away the moles!"

The farmer, in disbelief, was amazed. So the fox continued: "I know how to keep the moles away; if I can, I ask you to give me a bunch of grapes a day as a reward".

The farmer, recovering from the surprise, thought about it and said, "All right, fox. You are cunning, but this time I want to trust you. I would rather give you a bunch of grapes a day than see my beloved vineyard ruined forever by moles!"

"We have a deal!", said the fox, "I will come back when everything is ready".

So the fox returned to the woods and that same day began to put her plan into practice.

She knew that there was a language for the blind: "It is called Braille language, I studied it at school some time ago".

The fox took all the books that contained information about the language for the blind, studied them thoroughly and moved on to the second phase of her plan.

She took the farmer's signs and began to carve many dots into the wood, which are the letters of the Braille alphabet. In fact, those who are blind pass their paw over these dots and so they can finally understand what is written on them.

The idea of the fox was ingenious and, as soon as it was finished, she carried the sign on the edge of the fence, called the farmer and together they waited.

After a few minutes, a mole emerged who, passing her paw over the sign, finally managed to read: 'Vineyard, moles are forbidden entry'. And so, without saying anything, he left.

The farmer could not believe his eyes, the fox had been right!

"Fox, you did it, you found the solution to my problem! You really deserved this grape!", the farmer said, handing her a juicy bunch. "From now on, come to me and you will have your reward".

From that moment on, the fox did not even have to make an effort to get to the grapes: it was the farmer who offered them to her every day.

"Children, I am very fond of this story because it has a lesson that you must never forget. Honesty always wins over dishonesty," Papa Bear said seriously.

"Sooner or later the farmer would have caught the fox and there would never be any grapes for her to eat again. Always remember: dishonesty has a short life and does not allow you to sleep peacefully...like the sleep that you are going to have soon, my little ones!", he said, cuddling the twins.

"Papa, did the fox receive the grapes every day?", Ni asked.

"Of course, my love. And this is the second lesson of the story: solve a problem and you will be rewarded. The bigger the problem and the more you help others, the more you will be rewarded for your work," Papa Bear said, getting up and leaving the room.

"Now go to sleep and sweet dreams: a beautiful day awaits us tomorrow!"

"Good night, Papa," Ni and Vi replied.

The next day, Ni and Vi were very happy. "Papa, Papa! We dreamed about your stories! I dreamed about Aki and Vi dreamed about Naja".

"I am happy, it means that you liked the stories... and I, on the other hand, dreamed of the fox!" Papa Bear replied, laughing.

"Kids!" Mama Bear called from the kitchen, "come to the table, breakfast is ready! If you are good, while you eat I will tell you a story!"

"Wow!!" the twins said, running towards the kitchen.

After having breakfast, Mama Bear said: "And here we are, since you were good, I will tell you the story of a donkey so stubborn as to succeed in an extraordinary undertaking"...

The story of Giorgio:
the donkey who competed with horses

A long time ago Giorgio lived in Greece, a little donkey with a passion for racing and speed.

His house was full of images of famous race horses of the past; every day he looked at them and thought: "I will also compete as a great racer and I will be a champion!"

And so Giorgio began to train every day and, growing up, he became the fastest of all the donkeys.

But that was not enough for him, he wanted to compete with horses!

So he went to the racecourse and, to his general amazement, began to warm up to start his training.

"A donkey has never been seen to train with us," said Dago, the most famous and feared of coaches.

The horses began to laugh amongst themselves and make fun of Giorgio: "Come on, show us what you can do, donkey, you wouldn't want to disappoint us!".

And so the donkey got into position and left, but, due to the emotion, he stumbled, falling disastrously. All the horses laughed out loud and then Dago said, "Mule, maybe it's better if you go and transport bags of potatoes, instead of wasting our time!"

Giorgio, stubborn and touchy, turned to the horses and shouted, offended: "I'll show you! In a year I'll compete in the Big Race and you'll eat my dust!"

Our donkey then started working even harder. He trained all day, studied running techniques and read the stories of the great champions.

In a short time, he not only knew and applied all the existing running techniques, but he invented new ones, eager to try and try again.

Months passed and the donkey kept his promise by signing up for the Big Race, the most famous and prestigious race in all of Greece.

The long-awaited day arrived and Giorgio entered the stadium and positioned himself at the starting point next to the horses. Everyone in the stadium was amazed to see a donkey participate in the Big Race.

Everything was ready, the race was about to begin, the judge began the countdown: 3...2...1...GO!

Donkey started the biggest race of his life well: the horses looked at him in disbelief and there was a standing ovation for him from the audience.

Giorgio was fast and sped along with the leading group, but in the middle of the race the horses lengthened their pace and our donkey, with his small muscles and short legs, began to slow down instead.

Everyone overtook him and Giorgio, stumbling, closed the last race several seconds late.

Giorgio was very sad: he had worked so much that no one knew more about racing than him, and yet it was not enough!

The whole audience applauded him: he was still the fastest donkey they had ever seen, but he did not care.

Leaving the stadium, Giorgio passed Dago. "You were good, but you are not a horse, at most you can transport potatoes faster!" he said, laughing mockingly.

Donkey's confidence was shot and so he returned home with his ears down and his tail between his legs, but while he was at home crying, he heard a knock on the door.

When he opened, he saw a young horse who said: "Hi, Giorgio, my name is Lucky, I saw your race and I have to congratulate you."

"Don't make fun of me!" replied the donkey.

"I'm not making fun of you. I have never seen anyone run with your technique and I would like you to train me".

"You want me to train you? I'm not a coach, why don't you get trained by Dago like everyone else?"

"Because that way I would be one of the many and instead I feel that you would be the right coach for me. I want to be unique, like you!" he said enthusiastically.

Giorgio stopped to take a good look at him. "Hmmm," he thought, "he's young and teeny-tiny, but with the right training he could do it. I want to give him a chance!"

"All right, Lucky, I'll train you! But you will have to follow all my instructions. If you don't listen to me, I will no longer be your coach. We start tomorrow at dawn," Giorgio said sternly.

Giorgio launched himself into this undertaking with all the passion he possessed and subjected Lucky to all the training and all the techniques he had applied on himself.

Another year passed and this time, at the starting line of the Great Race, there was Lucky: he had become a powerful and muscular horse. His opponent was Lightning, the strongest horse trained by Dago.

After a close fight, Lucky began to lengthen his pace, using Giorgio's strategies, and crossed the finish line first. The absolute winner was Lucky, his student!

Giorgio began to shed great tears, but this time they were tears of happiness. Instead, there was nothing left for Dago but to congratulate Lucky and his coach with gritted teeth.

Lucky went on to win many more races, and Giorgio?

Our donkey became the most successful trainer in history, training many other horses over the years.

Soon Giorgio replaced the images of the glorious horses of his home's past with those of other racing legends. Those of his horses.

"Mama, what a super-mega-galactic story!", Ni said, almost jumping out of the chair in her enthusiasm.

"Yes, the story of our donkey is incredible and has several lessons. The first is that we must respect our nature. Giorgio was a wonderful donkey, but he was not equipped with the right muscles to compete. You see, my loves, competition can be very hard. That's why it's important to know your strengths and work hard on them to improve them, so you have a better chance of winning."

"I don't understand, Mom," said Ni.

"Each of us has qualities that allow us to excel with hard work. But at the same time we have weaknesses. If we ignore them, we risk spending years without concluding anything, because we have not given ourselves the opportunity to express our true abilities to the fullest. Only then will the odds play in our favor."

"But, Mom, Giorgio later became a great coach," replied Vi.

"You are right, Vi, Giorgio knew everything about running: he was passionate, intelligent, studious and a great worker, but he was not suitable for running. And this brings us to the second lesson of the story. You can never know when what you have learned will lead you to success. What you have to do is continue to learn new skills. Life is a continuous school. What Giorgio learned during his years of training allowed him to later become a great coach."

"It's true, Mom," the little bears replied.

"Also, do not be afraid of defeats, that's where the best turning points for your life come from. Always have faith in the future," concluded Mama Bear.

"Little ones, it's time to go to school. This afternoon, two more stories await you, as long as you are good and eat all the honey I have given you," Papa Bear said.

So Ni and Vi left the house and, skipping happily, they walked towards the school.

That afternoon the little twins were ready for a new story, so Papa Bear sat down in his large chair, with Vi and Ni on his lap, and said, "My little ones, now I will tell you the story of two little bunnies and their invention..."

The story of Roby and Toby and the carrot wheel.

Roby and Toby were two bunnies, great friends and great carrot lovers; but gathering carrots was really tiring!

"Toby, carrots are so tasty, I would never get tired of eating them!", Roby said.

"Yes, but they are also so difficult to pick from the ground, at the end of the day I am so exhausted that I do not have the strength to eat them!" Toby sighed.

"We need a tool to help us dig up our sweet carrots," Roby said thoughtfully.

"Yes, but nothing like that exists," Toby replied.

"Hey Toby, what if we invented it ourselves? We could pick carrots in a short time and easily, and we would eat so many that we would turn orange!" Roby exclaimed.

"I am coming up with a brilliant idea: in the vegetable garden the carrots are planted in rows and at an equal distance from each other. What if we created a wheel that, as it turned, picked carrots in our place?", Roby suggested.

Toby added: "We can mount pliers on it, so that as the wheel rolls, it grabs the carrots and rips them out of the ground."

"Yes, and also a nice large basket to gather them up in would be magnificent! Toby, we have to start building our wheel right away!" Roby shouted.

Toby was a little hesitant. He was shier than Roby, who on the other hand threw himself headlong into every new situation.

That's why Toby said, "Roby, wait, why don't we study all the books necessary to create our wheel first? We have to become blacksmiths, carpenters, mechanics and carrot experts, calculate the force required to pull a carrot, the size of the wheel and many other things..."

"Toby, if we do that, it will be months before we are ready! Whenever we have a problem, we could ask for advice from those who are more experienced than us, or look up books only as we need. "Come on, Toby, let's start building our wheel tomorrow!", Roby exclaimed.

Toby was always undecided and afraid of failing, so he said, "Roby, let's split up. You start building your wheel, and meanwhile I will make mine when I feel ready!"

So Roby, disappointed in his friend's choice, returned home and thought: "Starting tomorrow morning I will dedicate myself to building the most beautiful, resistant, and efficient wheel ever seen. It will be so fast that I will call it the Turbo-Carota".

In the morning, Roby got up and went to the carpenter, who advised him to use oak wood because it would be the most resistant. Roby went to the woods to collect all the wood necessary for his Turbo-Carota, while in the evening he studied books on how to build it.

Roby then went to the blacksmith to create the iron structure of his machine and later studied how to nail the oak wood boards to it.

In the meantime, Toby had finished reading the first book, How to Become a Good Carpenter, thus wasting precious days.

Roby, for his part, wanted to test the wheel immediately, even though it was far from being completed. He took it to the garden and began to roll it.

With great astonishment, Roby noticed that the wooden wheel was dented as it rolled on the ground. So he studied the problem and decided that he would add rubber to the edges of the wheel, to make it more resistant.

"My Turbo-Carrot will be unstoppable: no hole and no stone will be able to stop it!" Roby shouted.

What about Toby? He was in the middle of the book Everything you need to know to become a blacksmith: from A to Z.

After many changes and attempts, Roby finally made his Turbo-Carota wheel.

Roby went to call his friend Toby, who could not believe his eyes: the wheel was beautiful and very different from the initial project!

"How did you do it?", Toby asked, rubbing his eyes in disbelief.

"I learned gradually, learning from my mistakes." "I studied the topics that interested me and I got help from the carpenter, the blacksmith and the tire dealer...I tried and tried again, working day and night, and here is the wheel!", Roby replied.

Then Roby asked, "Do you like it? I call it the Turbo-Carota!"

"Yes, very much!" said Toby, a little envious. "Give it a try, let's see if it works!"

So Roby placed the wheel on the row of carrots and rolled it.

To the great astonishment of the bunnies, it worked!

The Turbo-Carota rolled and the pliers caught the carrots, extracting them from the ground without difficulty and then collecting them in a basket, ready to be eaten by the greedy bunnies.

It was at this point that Toby bitterly admitted, "Roby, you were right. I should have started working with you on the wheel right away. I just lost so much time without achieving anything concrete. The fear of failing paralyzed me".

Roby put a paw on his friend's shoulder and, smiling, said to him, "I'm glad you learned your lesson. Without action, ideas are just a dream."

"What a great idea, the Turbo-Carota!", Vi exclaimed.

"Roby and Toby were two very ingenious bunnies but, as poor Toby understood at his expense, an idea without implementation does not count for much. Always remember that, my children".

"Yes, Papa," Ni and Vi replied in unison.

"The second lesson is that you must be ready to change your initial plans. You may have to modify your project several times until it works perfectly. But it will not be a problem if you are flexible and ready to adapt".

It's true, Papa, Roby made so many changes to the Turbo-Carota!", Ni observed.

"Right, Ni. You are two insightful little bears and, to reward you, I will tell you a story that will take us back to Africa, more precisely to Madagascar..."

The story of the lemurs of Madagascar: when change means salvation.

Lemurs live in the forests of Madagascar: they are cute little animals similar to monkeys.

The lemurs climb trees and jump with great leaps from one branch to another to look for the leaves, their main source of food.

But due to the lengthening periods of drought, the lemurs were in serious danger because they risked having nothing to eat.

For this reason, the leaders of the two most important tribes met to discuss the problem and find a solution: Kito from the northern tribe and Delilah from the southern tribe.

Kito began to speak: "Delilah, the situation is serious: soon the leaves may be scarce."

Delilah came from the southern forest, the area most affected by the scorching climate: "The situation is even more serious with us, our stocks will not last more than a week and we do not know how long this great heat will last!"

Delilah had one more reason to be worried: she had recently become the mother of little Naki, a very sweet little bundle of fur.

So Delilah continued: "Kito, our tribe has decided to move. We can no longer passively remain in our lands and risk our lives".

Surprised, Kito said, "We lemurs have never left our home forest and for generations, we have always lived among the same trees. Changing is too risky!"

Then Delilah replied: "You are right, but our ancestors have always had enough leaves to survive the dry seasons. The drought is lasting longer and longer, so it is more risky to stay here, waiting for a rain that is not coming."

"And where would you like to go?", Kito asked.

"We will move to the end of the forest, to the rock fortress. In the shade of the high rocky mountains there are trees and leaves in abundance," Delilah replied.

"You've gone crazy! The rock fortress is a labyrinth of high, sharp peaks like blades. There are risks everywhere: if you miss a jump, you will end up in the ravines! Not to mention our predators: on the rocks, you'll be exposed to their attacks," Kito replied.

But Delilah and all her tribe had made a decision, so she replied: "Tomorrow we will leave towards our hope of salvation. If you want, you can join us".

Kito had no intention of risking it: he preferred to rely on the hope of the return of the rains. So Kito greeted Delilah and returned to his forest.

The next day the tribe led by Delilah was ready to leave, little Naki clung to her mother's back and all together they started.

With great leaps, the lemurs jumped from one branch to another until they reached the foot of the imposing mountains.

Before starting the climb, the lemurs stopped to look at it from the top of the trees: the high, rocky peaks loomed threateningly, so sharp that they could even slice the sky in two.

At one point, while they were standing there and afraid to observe the majesty of the mountains, Delilah saw a green patch: "Hey all of you, look over there! There is a tree full of leaves waiting for us! Come on, let's climb this first peak," she shouted, giving strength to the group.

The lemurs began to climb easily and, when they reached the top, they saw something unimaginable: in the distance, in the center of that labyrinth of rocks, there was a green forest ready to welcome them.

But to reach it they would have to jump from one peak to another with the utmost caution. Kito was right:

the rocks were sharp like blades and a slight mistake would have been enough to seriously injure oneself.

Delilah was the tribe leader, so it was her turn to jump first and it was even more difficult for her because she had the weight of her daughter Naki on her shoulders.

Each movement had to be calculated with millimeter precision because, between one peak and another, there were deep ravines: a single missed step could prove fatal for both.

But her love for her daughter gave her the necessary strength and so, with the whole herd watching, Delilah made the first leap and began to enter the labyrinth of rocks.

The other lemurs began to follow her and with each leap they felt more and more secure, but, halfway through, they heard large birds flying over the area.

These ugly raptors were fearsome enemies, so now the lemurs had to hurry: noon had long passed and the sun would soon set, putting them in serious danger.

So the herd began to hurry and, peak after peak, jump after jump, the lemurs came closer and closer to the promised land.

Tired and exhausted, just as the sun disappeared on the horizon, Delilah made the last leap and put little Naki safely on a tree.

It seemed impossible and yet they had made it: they had arrived in a lush forest full of juicy leaves, ready to be eaten.

Delilah had never been so happy: she had saved the future of her tribe and of little Naki.

The southern lemurs had faced a long and tiring journey, full of pitfalls and dangers, but having left their native forest was their salvation.

"Kids, this story is about the importance of change," Papa Bear said.

"It's true, Papa," observed Ni.

Papa Bear replied: "It may happen that what gives you nourishment runs out, just like our lemurs' leaves. If it happens, do not waste time despairing and regretting the past but, on the contrary, immediately work to find a new path. The world is so full of opportunities!"

"Papa, the lemurs were very brave!", Vi said.

"Exactly, Vi. You see, change is scary because we do not know what awaits us on the other side. It is more comfortable to live in our usual forest, but remember: our roots nourish us, but they can also hold us back".

"Papa, what happened to the other tribe?", Ni asked.

"The tribe of Kito did not move, even when the last leaf fell, so many lemurs could not survive the dry season," Papa Bear replied sadly.

"We're so sorry for them!", Ni and Vi said.

Papa Bear wanted his children to fully understand the lesson: "Yes, my loves, this story teaches us not to wait until it is too late to change. Changes are your friends if you can face them with the right courage".

"And now, before dinner, I will tell you a story that happened in the wilds of Alaska that dates back to the time of your great-great-grandfather".

It was told to me by my father when I was little and now I will tell it to you two so that you can treasure his lesson".

The story of the poor carpenter and the golden apple orchard.

Alaska is a distant land with unspoilt nature made up of rivers, lakes, forests and...golden apples!

Some time ago, some explorer bears discovered trees in Alaska that produced large and shiny apples made of the precious metal. When the news spread, bears began to arrive from everywhere, attracted by the possibility of collecting so many golden apples that they would no longer have to work for the rest of their lives.

At that time there lived a bear named Bruno, a humble carpenter who wanted more than anything to give a better life to his three little bears, so, together with his entire family, he too left, full of hope, for Alaska.

The golden apple orchard was not an easily accessible place: on the contrary, it was necessary to cross impetuous rivers, disruptive waterfalls, impenetrable forests and long winding paths, but, after a thousand vicissitudes, our carpenter and his family managed to reach their destination.

As soon as Bruno arrived, he noticed that the golden apples were very difficult to collect, because they grew only on the tops of very high trees. And then there were also many competitors who tried to reach the apples, but without success.

In fact, the big bears were so clumsy and heavy that they could not climb the trees and so the apples continued to gleam mockingly in the sky and there was nothing left for the gold seekers but to look at them with their noses upturned.

Bruno was the only one who had brought tools with him: a hammer, an axe, a saw and many nails to build a hut for his family; while the other bears had nothing, because they had wanted to travel light and get to the golden apple orchard quickly.

This was the luck of the poor carpenter, who, observing the bears in difficulty, thought: "All these bears do not know how to reach the apples, they need stairs and I am the only one able to manufacture them within a radius of hundreds of kilometers!"

So he explained his idea to the family and, together, they went into the forest where they would find wood in abundance. Working day and night and resting only for a few hours, Bruno and his family cut and assembled dozens and dozens of stairs without stopping.

The ingenious carpenter also devised sticks with a net at the end made of interwoven roots to easily collect the apples by extending only one paw.

When Bruno had built enough stairs and sticks, he returned again to the golden apple orchard and, climbing on a rock, drew the attention of the bears towards himself.

"Attention, bears, I am here to help you!", he shouted with all the power in his lungs.

The bears turned their eyes away from the golden apples and, intrigued, gathered under the rock where the carpenter was standing, as he continued: "Are you tired of just looking at the golden apples?
Do you finally want to collect them?",
he asked, already knowing the answer.

"Yessss!!" all the bears replied
in unison.

Bruno now had their complete
attention: "I have the solution
for you: I have built all the stairs
you see here next to me.

In addition, I also made sticks to allow you to pick the apples comfortably and effortlessly!"

To the bears it did not seem true, they already imagined themselves on the trees picking apples and from the crowd there were cries of: "Bravo! That's just what we need, how can we get them?"

The carpenter felt that he had them in the palm of his hand and seized the opportunity, answering: "Of course! But in return I ask you for one golden apple for every four you collect".

The bears looked amazed: they were not expecting such a request and did not know what to answer.

"Without my stairs," said Bruno, noting their hesitation, "you will not have any apples and you will be forced to return home empty-handed. Is that what you want? I don't think so. Therefore, with my proposal we all win: you will have the much-desired apples and I will be rewarded for my work. What do you think?"

Finally, a large bear came forward from the group who, without uncertainty, shook the carpenter's hand, saying: "My friend, we have a deal! At the end of the day, we will count the apples and you will have what you need".

At that point the other bears, fearing that the apples might run out, crowded to conclude the agreement with Bruno and in a short time everyone got to work: dozens of bears climbed and descended their stairs at full speed, stretching their sticks to collect as many apples as possible.

The carpenter, from time to time, had to intervene to fix some broken stairs or fix a stick that had been broken by a clumsy bear, but soon his efforts would bear fruit...golden fruit!

In fact, as the bears collected the golden apples from the trees, rows of sacks were filled with precious apples, which were just waiting to be counted.

When there was no longer a single apple glittering in the sky, all the bears divided the loot as agreed and the carpenter received one apple for every four apples harvested.

When Bruno finished counting his reward, he rubbed his eyes in disbelief: in a single day he had obtained hundreds of golden apples, more than he would ever be able to collect in weeks of work!

Our no-longer-poor carpenter finally had so many apples that he no longer had to worry about his future and that of his family.

As soon as the story was finished, the voice of Mama Bear was heard: "Kids, dinner is ready, everyone come and eat!"

Papa Bear, not wanting to make Mom angry, hurriedly explained to the children: "Kids, did you like this story?"

"Yes, Papa, very much!", Ni and Vi replied.

"It contains an important lesson: if a large number of bears jump headlong into a new adventure, perhaps the best way is to provide the necessary tools instead of joining them. Follow the Bruno's example, the bear who gave stairs and sticks to those who wanted golden apples".

"I would never have thought of it, Papa," Ni exclaimed.

"Because, Ni, thinking differently requires habit and training, but you will also be able to, I am sure," Papa Bear said, patting the heads of his little twins.

But the lessons were not over, in fact Papa Bear continued: "If you want to be successful in your initiatives, you will have to learn to persuade others to convince them of the strength of your ideas, just as the carpenter did by climbing the rock and talking to the crowd of bears".

But at that point, Mama Bear was again heard shouting in an angrier tone: "Kids!!"

Papa Bear, knowing that he had gotten under her skin, said, "Come on, let's go to dinner. Tonight, when you are in bed, I will tell you the last of my stories".

Later on, Papa Bear and Mama Bear went up to the twins' room to tell them the last story, as promised.

Ni and Vi were filled with excitement and curiosity.

"This is the story of a little mouse who had a big idea..."

The story of Ralph, the miner who left his mine.

Ralph was a smart little cheese-mining mouse.

Our Ralph woke up when the sky was still dark, went to the mine to dig the precious cheese shavings and finished picking when the sun was already setting.

Ralph could get about ten shavings of cheese a day: it was a very hard job, but one that was necessary to feed his family, which had expanded with the arrival of his little mice.

Precisely because of the need to have more space for himself and his family, Ralph, after returning one night from the mine, began to dig to create a more comfortable den.

Instead, all the other mice in the colony slept side by side or in the narrow tunnels created by the miners in the mine.

Ralph was a hard worker and a good builder, so within a few weeks he had created a large den suitable to house his little ones.

One day, Ralph showed his new home to his friends Freddie and Jerry, who were impressed by its beauty.

Ralph had created a room with straw to sleep in, an area where he could eat, a pantry where he could store cheese and another where he could...do his business in peace!

His friend Freddie said in amazement, "Ralph, you have a beautiful house, you have a talent for building dens. I would pay to be in a place like this, instead of living in those narrow tunnels".

"I would pay too, I like your house so much!" Jerry confirmed

"It takes commitment, but you can do it too. Every night I dug after work and created all the rooms you see," Ralph explained to them.

"Come on, Ralph, you're a more experienced digger than we are, and then in the evening we're so tired that we don't want to go back to work..." Freddie and Jerry replied.

Ralph, at this point, had an idea: "What if I built a house for you, just like this? Could you give me some of the cheese you collect in the mine: how about one shaving of cheese a day?", Ralph ventured.

"Let's see...we mice collect ten shavings every day, giving you one to live comfortably in a house like this seems to me a fair exchange. All right, Ralph, you will make a den where I can live with my family and in return I will give you one shaving of cheese a day," Freddie said, shaking his paw.

"That's fine with me too," Jerry followed.

And so the small miner began to dig alone, always in the evening and after working in the mine, to make the two houses the same as his.

It was a hard time for our Ralph: he would have wanted so much to rest with his wife and play with his little ones. Instead, he finished working late at night, returning home when everyone was already asleep, resting for only a few hours and returning to the mine at dawn for another hard day.

Several times Ralph was on the verge of giving up, but he knew that, once the job was finished, he could guarantee two extra shavings of cheese to his family. So he held on and, after a few months, he handed the two dens over to his friends.

Freddie and Jerry were so happy with the comfort of their new homes that not only did they start paying Ralph on time with one shaving of cheese a day, but they talked about it with such enthusiasm to family, friends and acquaintances, that in a short time our little mouse received orders for eight more new dens.

Ralph was very happy with his success, but also very tired: he could not go on working all day in the mine and then continuing to dig in the evening.

So his wife gave him some advice: "Ralph, work only for half a day in the mine, until you have finished the new dens, so you will have more time to complete them. You can also get help from some miners, paying for it with our cheese reserves. After all, you have always worked hard up to now and we can afford it".

"You're right, by following your advice I will be able to complete all the houses in half the time," Ralph replied.

Ralph went to work with renewed energy and, thanks to the help of the mining friends he had hired, he completed all the promised houses.

At the end of all his labors, Ralph could count on a total of ten shavings of cheese, paid every day by those who used his dens.

That was the same amount of cheese that he made on a daily basis and with so much hard work in the mine!

Meanwhile, Ralph's dens were increasingly successful and our little mouse continued to receive orders for new houses every day.

Now Ralph felt free to follow his new passion: he left the job in the mine and dedicated himself fully to creating new dens that were increasingly beautiful and comfortable.

Ralph was only a small cheese miner like many others, but he had come a long way: now he was the master of his destiny and he no longer had to get the cheese in the mine.

"Papa, this story is my favorite!", said Vi.

"Yes, but Ralph had to do so much hard work!", observed Ni.

"You are both right, my little ones. Now that we are at the end of my stories, you will have noticed that hard work is present in all the stories," Papa Bear commented.

"But then Ralph could leave that tough job in the mine and spend more time with his family," said Vi thoughtfully.

"That's right, I see that you have understood the lesson: your future will depend on what you do today and the effort you put into your present!" Papa Bear replied.

Seeing his little ones begin to yawn, Papa Bear turned off the light, wished them good night and, closing the door of their room, stopped to think: "Who knows if the seeds of my stories will take root in their minds...".

The next day, Ni and Vi were more cheerful than usual and, running through the woods, they remembered the stories of their new heroes: Ralph, Aki, Naja, Delilah, etc.

"Papa, you promised to tell us your story, too," the little twins said at one point.

"I thought you had forgotten: you don't miss a trick! Every promise must be kept, therefore ..."

The story of Papa Bear and his two inventions.

Kids, I started by studying the stories I have told you to understand how I can use their teachings to my advantage.

While I was working in the woods, I began to think about how I could improve the lives of the other bears and suddenly it became clear to me what I could do to help them collect honey.

We bears have to fight every time against the bees that defend their honey, and so that's where the first idea came from: to invent something that attracts the bees out of the hive in order to avoid their painful stings.

Then I noticed that, while we were trying to detach a hive from the tree, it often escaped from our paws, falling to the ground and shattering into many pieces.

In short, a great nuisance and a great waste of honey, so I had the second idea: to make a tool to detach and collect the hives easily.

I talked about what I wanted to achieve to my friends, but they took me for a fool: "We have always done this, why do you want to change?", they told me.

It felt as if I was hearing the story of Naja the gazelle, and that's why I didn't listen to them. I could already see my inventions in my head, like the little monkey Aki who saw his pool where others could only see a steep slope. Besides, my mother believed in me and that was enough for me.

I needed inspiration to put my ideas in motion, but in Honey Wood there was nothing that could help me, so I left for distant places to discover different ways of collecting honey.

I travelled for a long time, a bit like the lemurs of Madagascar did, and in the end I arrived at Beehive Town, where I discovered that the bears used smoke to stun the bees.

But the smoke also created panic among the poor bees, who remained confused for a long time, so I thought of the story of the fox: on the contrary, I wanted to invent an honest way to move the bees away without traumatizing them.

That's how I began to have the idea for the 1000Flowers Perfume, a concentrate of the best flowers in our forest, so irresistible for bees that they voluntarily move away from the hive, without any harm to them.

I went back on the road and after some time I arrived at the village of Bear Wood, where the hives were collected by shaking them with a stick, often breaking them, unfortunately.

That scenario led me to come up with the 2in1 Stick, which would have a pliers to detach the hive, and then roll it into a basket attached right at the end of the stick, without damage.

I returned home with my ideas and, drawing on the lesson of the bunnies Roby and Toby, I immediately got to work: I talked to experts on flowers, bees and perfumes, I met carpenters, blacksmiths and mechanics and then I bought the books I needed to learn what I still did not know.

During the day I went to work and in the evening, until late at night, I would devote myself to my project, just like the little mouse Ralph. I do not deny that it was a hard time, but one that was also very beautiful and exciting, which I still remember with nostalgia.

There were many unforeseen events, as happened with the landslide in Aki and I was mocked, as happened to Giorgio, the coaching donkey. But I hung on, and in the end my inventions were ready to be tested.

So Mama Bear sprayed the 1000Flowers Perfume on a meadow far from the hive we wanted to take and the bees found its fragrance so irresistible, that they voluntarily moved away from the hive, which I then easily collected with the 2in1 Stick.

We were very happy because, after so much effort, the two ideas worked wonderfully.

At this point I had to propose my inventions to the other bears, just as Bruno did with the golden apples.

At first they were all a little suspicious, but when they saw the 1000Flowers Perfume and the 2in1 Stick in action, no one had any more doubts: in fact, they were so enthusiastic that they wanted to start using them immediately!

So I proposed a similar agreement to that of the little mouse Ralph and, for each month of using my two inventions, each bear would give me a jar of honey.

The bears accepted because it was a fair exchange for everyone: no one would be stung by the bees anymore and the honey would no longer be spilt on the ground: instead they would collect it easily until the last drop.

I had solved two problems by making the lives of the other bears more comfortable and easier and for this I was rewarded, just as happened to the fox with its grapes.

Since then we have had plenty of honey, I no longer have to get up early to go and collect it and I can spend more time with you, my little ones.

So remember: if you want a better life, first you have to make the lives of others better.

"Papa, you are our hero!" the twins shouted in unison.

"No, kids: I'm a bear like the others. I only had a dream and the courage and determination to achieve it," Papa Bear replied modestly.

"Papa, were you never discouraged?", Ni asked.

"Far from it Ni, I had so many doubts that I was on the verge of abandoning everything and returning to my previous life. But I had two little bears as a motivation and in addition your mother has always supported me, even in the most difficult moments", Papa Bear replied.

"So, Papa, does an entrepreneur solve people's problems?", Vi asked.

"Exactly, the world is full of entrepreneurs who improve the lives of others, do you want some other examples?"

"Yes, Papa!", the twins said.

So Papa Bear continued "Well, here are a few examples.

You know the story of the three little pigs. Do you know what they do now? They build houses with cameras and anti-intrusion systems to drive away hungry wolves; no one dares to enter their homes anymore.

Hansel and Gretel? They are no longer attracted to evil witches because now they own the best sweets factory in the world!

And Little Red Riding Hood, who wandered alone in the woods? She learned her lesson and has a bodyguard company to escort helpless girls to their grandmothers' houses safe and sound.

Rapunzel, the princess with the long braid? She has created her very successful line of hair cosmetics. She bought a beautiful one-story house so that her prince charming no longer has to climb her hair, but only has to ring a bell.

The beautiful Snow White? She founded a large beauty center called "The Most Beautiful in the Realm", so even stepmothers can be beautiful and no longer be envious.

Cinderella? She has a chain of shoe stores. The glass slippers were really uncomfortable, so she created her own line of comfortable and fashionable shoes.

In short, my loves, you have already understood that ideas are everywhere. Let yourself be inspired by the world, change what you do not like, make life easier for others, solve the problems of others and you will be rewarded.

In addition, you will live with the satisfaction of having created something that was not there, of having had an idea that others did not have, and of having helped to advance the world a little. You have the precious opportunity to make a difference in life, do not waste it!", Papa Bear concluded.

The twins were enchanted by their father's speech and when they finished listening to him, they began to run and jump happily, fantasizing:

"I will become an entrepreneur, I will invent a way to preserve honey for longer!", said Ni.

"I, on the other hand, will find a way to help the bees build the hive faster!" replied Vi.

Mama Bear had seen the whole scene, approached Papa Bear and, surprising him with a hug, said: "There you go, Max, you have also infected them with your enthusiasm. I wonder if they will become entrepreneurs?"

At that point Papa Bear cast a loving look at his twins, sighed and said, "Tracy, in their lives they can do anything they want. But, in the depths of my heart, I hope so".

Massimo Dambrosio

An entrepreneur and father of twins, he is passionate about personal growth and inspired by the teachings of great entrepreneurs such as MJ De Marco, Warren Buffett, Charlie Munger, and Phil Knight. With this book, he wanted to pass on to his children the values that have guided him not only in his work but also in his life.

Made in the USA
Columbia, SC
07 December 2024

48691888R00052